ALASKAN WILDLIFE

ALASKAN WILDLIFE

PHOTOGRAPHY BY TOM WALKER
TEXT BY MARYDITH BEEMAN

✖ GRAPHIC ARTS CENTER PUBLISHING COMPANY, PORTLAND, OREGON

International Standard Book Number 0-932575-29-3
Library of Congress Catalog Number 86-83244
Copyright © MCMLXXXVII by
Graphic Arts Center Publishing Company
P.O. Box 10306 • Portland, Oregon 97210 • (503) 226-2402
Editor-in-Chief • Douglas A. Pfeiffer
Designer • Robert Reynolds
Typographer • Harrison Typesetting, Inc.
Printer • Graphic Arts Center
Bindery • Lincoln & Allen
Printed in the United States of America

Special Consultant on Wildlife:
Dr. Robert Weeden
Professor of Resource Management
Biology, Fisheries, and Wildlife Department
University of Alaska–Fairbanks

■ *Frontispiece*: Deer antlers are shed yearly, but the horns of mountain sheep stay throughout life. The age of Dall sheep, *Ovis dalli*, is calculated by counting the darker, coarser rings which are set in the horns when horn growth slows and stops yearly at the fall rut. Ewes have much shorter, thinner horns, but both are light colored.

Alaska's rare winter visitor from the Soviet Union is the whooper swan, *Olor cygnus*.

At birth, harbor seals, *Phoca vitulina*, weigh about twenty-five pounds; by maturity, two hundred.

INTRODUCTION

Beyond the cities and towns of Alaska lie valleys where streams run clean, mountainsides where downed airplanes rest undiscovered, and forests where few human shadows have been cast. In imagination or in actuality, some of us seek out these places. They may be lonely or wild or even desolate. Nevertheless, we want to be the first ones there—or the last.

What is it about Alaska that sparks the primitive in us? It is not just the land, laid down by old seas, cut and exposed by wind and water, twisted and contorted by earthquakes and volcanoes. Nor is it the seasons, characterized by long summer days or longer winter nights. It is not the storms thrown at the mainland from the North Pacific, nor the metallic cold which is cast in the air over Canada or Siberia. In Alaska, life responds to *life*.

Consider migrations: marine life for the bit of salt sea we carry within; birds for the Lindberghs in our souls; mammals whose patterns of wandering and migration mark the seasons as accurately as our holidays.

Consider displays: spruce grouse strutting like the lovers among us; a broken wing mirroring fears we have for our own young; a Dall ram presenting his stately horns to another ram, much as a man might flex his muscles in the face of a competitor.

Such similarities tempt us to assign human characteristics to animals, a practice which raises the hackles and bares the teeth of many biologists. "People are people," says an authority, "and bears are bears." And yet another expert says he thinks possibly mountain goats are displaying a sense of fun when they jump down an icy bank, flip sideways, and run zigzag in the snow. He calls it exuberance and adds wryly, "Maybe they do it for spiritual reasons." Maybe they do. So too can we respond to life and celebrate it in the great wild places of Alaska.

THE SONGS OF THE WOLVES

My personal celebration? One cold, winter night, I sang with the wolves.

Deep winter in the mountains is a time of peculiar tensions. The cold is so sharp, one waits for the wind to break it, bringing change. The dark hours are too many, poorly balanced by a mere pretense at day. In the evening, the silence is profound; one welcomes the sounds of a partner, a tinny radio, or even a friendly weasel.

One evening, I elbowed open the cabin door and backed out with a red plastic dishpan in my hands to meet a frigid bank of air. It curled, fog now, into the warm building before the door closed with a soft thud behind me. In the blackness I stepped a few paces and let fly. Water to ice crackled, freezing immediately to a low mound of spent dishwaters.

The night was breathtaking. I stole a moment to look up and discerned sky from earth only by a sifting of stars. Suddenly the night was charged by something out of place. I heard quick padding. Then came more muffled steps off to the right. Something was coming up the short hill from the frozen lake. Was it loose huskies? My son had five sled dogs that were tied up on the other side of the cabin. If a dog had slipped a collar, he would have approached me for warmth and a handout. These mysterious feet kept a distance.

Off to the left, one of the tethered dogs let out a nervous yip. The footsteps stopped about thirty feet away from me, on the edge of the woods.

"Pst!" I hissed at the family through a cracked-open door. "Wolves!" My husband extinguished the gas lanterns inside and joined me with the children.

At first, wolves and humans tested each others' silence. Then the song began, as one wolf voice started low, peaked, and then fell off. Another voice answered, or was it a statement of his own? It started at a higher pitch and was sustained until the tone broke off with a quaver. Then the others came in.

But now the bizarre occurred. From a mountain across the lake came the same song, tailing it by a split second. With a chill, I realized the hills themselves were howling! The dogs could no longer contain themselves and raised their voices with the first singers and their echoing ghost pack.

Last, and shiest of all, we humans began to howl under cover of darkness. "Owooooooooo!" Our first attempts were awkward, too tied up with human speech and tongue and teeth. I moved the sound back, visualizing it as if it were coming from the back of a high cave roof. In all the world as I know it, singing with the wolves is the wildest and most primitive of rites.

Now that I was a practiced singer, I was ready for embellishments. But the wolves were finished, and they took off into the woods. To expect such a thing to happen more than once in a lifetime is a kind of arrogance. But through the singing of such songs some of us appreciate that we *require* wild retreats. In Alaska we can find them.

THE FOREST FOR THE TREES

Almost every evening on television, weather satellite pictures show big pressure systems breaking like waves on Southeastern Alaska and her Gulf Coast. In November, moisture-soaked Aleutian clouds roll east. They are lifted and chilled by the mountains of the mainland and fall as wet, heavy snow. To a man sitting in a living room there is not much difference between two and three feet of snow, but to the Sitka black-tailed deer, the distinction is crucial. Generally, blacktails stay in the valley systems of their birth, traveling to high elevations in the summer and the lowlands in the cold weather. They are preyed upon by wolves and bears and are hunted by man. Their young may be taken by eagles. But their main enemy is that extra foot or more of snow.

From spring until fall, blacktails become fat from browsing on herbaceous growth. Their spring favorite, the skunk cabbage, is 15 to 20 percent protein. After the fall rut, or breeding season, feed freezes gradually as the snow moves down the mountains. Soon winter comes in earnest. In a normal winter, the numbers of deer are held in balance. In a mild one, an abundant blacktail population stays high, and ordinary winter fare may be overbrowsed. Then the drop of deer is precipitous. But when a severe winter comes, the movement of the deer is restricted, and perennial feed, such as ground dogwood, bramble, and goldthread, is buried. Only taller and nutritionally poorer browse like tough blueberry bushes remains exposed above the snow.

Gradually driven to the beaches by the deepening snow of late winter, the starving deer try to survive along a strip of tideland with its meager fare of kelp, dead grasses, and sedge. The first to die are the young, then the old, and then the weaker adults. Those who live on to the soft summer days ahead are the strongest ones.

Nature's population controls are sometimes harsh. Starvation is one. Fire can be another, but here in this damp climate, where rainfall may be in hundreds of inches annually, it is seldom felt. Man's activities, however, do affect the deer in Southeastern Alaska. Forest service personnel are studying heavy snow accumulation in the timber industry's clearcut areas and are comparing it with snow accumulation in old growth and thinned second growth forests to identify feeding and mobility patterns. Also, differing stages of forest growth are favorable to certain animals: bear, moose, deer, blue grouse, bald eagles, to name a few. Criticism of logging Southeastern must be tempered by the realization that after one hundred years have passed, only 12 percent of the Tongass National Forest will have been cut, and that will grow back. In fact, 5.5 million acres of the forest is wilderness-designated and is off limits to the timber industry.

Where wet coastal forests give way to transitional zones and inland habitat, tall trees vanish and forests open up. Here is a hybrid spruce called Lutz, a mixture of Sitka and white spruce, which is dominant on the Kenai Peninsula. Lutz spruces and hemlocks are found interspersed with smaller cottonwoods, birch, balsam poplar, aspen, and black spruce. The latter is a sorry-looking urchin that grows best in Alaska's worst soil. Farther north, tamaracks shed their needles in the fall. But without some of the state's thirty-six kinds of willows, the moose would not be so well fed.

The greatest concentrations of moose occur where willow is within reach. Black-tailed deer weigh between eighty and one hundred pounds, while many adult moose weigh half a ton or more, not the least part of it nose. Jokes about its protuberance cease, however, when a big bull comes into view. In the fall, during his prime, a bull's antlers can measure more than eighty inches across, wider by a foot than the breadth of a full-size car. Trophy hunters, hikers, and photographers value Alaska's estimated one hundred twenty thousand moose, but no more so than meat eaters. More than seven thousand moose per year are tucked away in freezers or hung from nails in meat houses. Moose meat is lower in cholesterol and fat than beef, is free from steroids, and like Everest, is *there*, in many cases, closer than the supermarket.

By September and October, moose that have not already been feeding in upland willow thickets may forsake their lowland summer habitat. They work their way up to timberline for the rut, a term which comes from the Latin *rugitus*, meaning bellowing. The bull's antlers, or "rack," which were draped a month before in peeling banners of velvet, have hardened by now. To the delicate or untrained observer, the bull's rutting behavior may seem somewhat uncouth. He digs a pit, urinates in it, drinks, tosses the softened turf, and rubs his shoulders in it. This apparently serves to ready him for mating. Bulls breed more than one cow each season. In the process, they expend large amounts of energy through incessant wandering and fighting with other bulls. By the time the mating season is over, bulls have lost much of their stored body fat. Bulls have been sighted at the end of the fall with their rib bones showing. Some experts think rutting bulls have a shorter life span because of it. Early cold and snow may make it impossible for the moose to recover the reserve of fat so necessary to winter survival.

When I first came north, the cafeteria in the school where I taught served moose meat as often as three times per week. Moose killed by cars were salvaged by the Territorial Police for us. Today, charities receive such bounty. A friend who lives near Palmer was under contract to remove all moose hit along a main highway. He found himself called out at all hours of the night like the vanishing country doctor. Highway planners who trained in other parts of the nation probably never thought they would be identifying moose crossings, but they meet with fish and game officials to plan roads, hoping to minimize such road kills.

Another hazard for moose is the engines of the Alaska Railroad. When snow is deep and crusted, moose frequent the long, plowed corridor of the rail bed. In the worst winters, hundreds are killed, and 90 percent of the meat is probably lost. Many solutions have been tried, but with little success. Fortunately, there are few roads and only one railroad in Alaska.

When the long, spring days return, moose life gets a bit easier. Moose calves that weigh about thirty pounds when they are born in late May or early June, fill out rapidly on milk and willow. By the time they are weaned in autumn, they have gained a prodigious three hundred pounds or more! At this rate of growth, a human baby of four months would tip the scales at ninety pounds.

Our understanding of wolf predation on moose has undergone modification in the last few years. It had been suggested that wolves were the major cause of mortality among sick or old moose. However, a study done recently at the Kenai National Moose Refuge on sixty radio-collared moose suggests otherwise. The animals were followed for several years, and none was lost to wolves. The years during which the study was made happened to have relatively mild winters with little snow. On the other hand, another study showed that wolves do kill moose on the Kenai. Of 206 moose killed by wolves, 47 percent were calves, and most of the rest were very old cows. Scientists now think that heavy, soft snow makes it easier for wolves to prey on moose. However, new findings in Southeast Alaska show moose can live there in snow depths of five feet, but only if the snow has a crust thick enough to support them. By taking cover under mature spruces, moose can also move where snow accumulation is less.

In spring and summer, moose browse on willow, birch, and aspen in the wild. They also like new shoots found on disturbed sites such as year-old rights-of-way, burns, and construction projects. Moose have been known to effectively prune prize landscaping. When the chain saws fell trees on power line right-of-ways on the Kenai Peninsula, it is not unusual to see moose in the clearings. The moose have learned to come here so that they can browse on the long-out-of-reach treetops. Near Anchorage, moose feed on grass along the highway, as fifty thousand cars speed to and from the city each day.

OTHER CREATURES OF THE FOREST

One foggy day I stopped at a lodge on the Anchorage-Glennallen Highway for a bite to eat. Parked outside was a tour bus. From my seat at the restaurant counter, I overheard an old gentleman complain: "We get on in Chicago. We drive all the way through hunerts of miles of Canada. Finally we get to Alaska. Trees, trees, nuttin' but trees."

The winter pelage of the snowshoe hare is camouflage only when against the snow.

Barren ground caribou battle in the breeding season during their move to wintering grounds.

The taiga, or boreal forest, lies in the subarctic between approximately sixty-two and sixty-eight degrees north latitude. Unmoderated by the sea's influence, this area truly becomes Mr. Seward's Ice Box in the winter. In the summer, temperatures climb into the nineties. This is the haunt of the black bear.

When he is walking, the average blackie reaches just about thigh or hip height on a human. When the black bear stands on his hind feet and sniffs the air, he resembles a six-footer at the airport searching the crowd for an arriving passenger.

These bears are very black indeed, and so belie tales such as one I heard in which a black bear went into a brush patch and came out a porcupine—an old joke based more on poor distance judging than color. Most have a small patch of white on their chest and a lightish muzzle.

The bear that humans encounter first is the black for two reasons: most human settlements are in wooded country where blacks are found; and blacks adapt more readily to people than do their larger cousins, the brown/grizzly bears. Black bears, in a rough estimate of twenty-five thousand, roam most of the forested areas of the vast mainland and some islands throughout the state. Brown and cinnamon phases are fewer in number; the "blue" or "glacier" bear is rarer still. The latter is usually found in a geographically isolated region along the Gulf of Alaska. Because of its isolation, the bear's color is perpetuated by a combining of recessive genes. Isolation may be a favorable influence for keeping this color, while hunting for that same trait may not; it could deplete the number of bears with that gene.

Experienced bear watchers prefer to keep this mammal at a safe distance, especially if the bear is a sow protecting her cubs. It is unlikely that black bears would seek out humans to fill their stomachs, but they do have a surprisingly varied diet. They eat fish, carrion, mussels, young mammals, and insects, but they rely most heavily on horsetails, other herbs, and berries. I once watched a black bear contentedly nuzzling and cropping his way through a blueberry patch. Suddenly a brown bear came on the scene. There was no fight; after a rush of brown, the black bear simply retreated into the trees, leaving the berries to the bigger bear.

Bears mate in summer, but within the mother, the fertilized egg remains unattached to the uterine wall for several months. If food is plentiful, the egg follows its normal course of development. But in times of meager rations, when a sow would not be able to feed her young adequately, her own undernourished body responds by spontaneously aborting the egg.

During January or February, one to four cubs are born in the den. They play and eat all summer, are weaned by the following fall, and den one more winter with the sow. The family dissolves in its second spring, with the sow ready for mating again.

If moose and bears command our respect because of their size, one of Alaska's smallest creatures, the weasel, does so because of its ferocity. People who live in remote areas regard the weasel highly. They say, "If the short-tailed weasel was the size of a wolverine, the woods would be too dangerous for me." This image of the weasel arises from his high-pitched activity as he kills and consumes an astonishing variety of prey: small mammals several times his size, insects, birds, and fish. He also takes eggs. Weasels measure a little more than a foot and weigh just half a pound, but their metabolism demands that they eat half their own weight

daily. (That would be like a teenager putting away seventy-five pizzas or so between dawn and dusk.) For this reason, the weasel is welcome in a cabin infested with mice.

The weasel changes names as his coat changes. In winter he is called an ermine. Because the demand for his fur has declined, the ermine now usually keeps his white fur coat to himself. I once tried to get a photo of a weasel in his royal garb, but he kept popping from one hole to another under the roots of some spruces. His quick, fluid motions have earned him a reputation as a slippery fellow, and thus his name has been incorporated into our language. In complaining to a biologist about the frequent use he and his colleagues made of words such as "usually," "generally," and "in most cases," I was told that these "weasel words" were necessary because biological data cannot be extrapolated from one situation to another.

Another small forest mammal is the red squirrel, thinner and of slighter stature than his gray cousin to the south. He lives in mature spruce woods and eats the seeds of cones. Squirrels are normally heard before they are seen, but they can be found by locating their nests, often made of grass and moss, but sometimes of sticks. These nests look like tree growths called "witches' brooms." Squirrel "middens," where the scales of cones have fallen, are also signs that squirrels are nearby. You know you are in squirrel country when you come upon dried mushrooms hanging seven feet from the ground. One winter, I discovered that one of my hip boots had been filled with mushrooms, either by red or flying squirrels. Although the mushrooms may be tempting to sample, they are the squirrel's cache. Some are also poisonous to humans.

The porcupine is an uninvited and unwanted visitor in any camp built of plywood. He has eaten many a door and crunched corners in the best of Alaskan bush dwellings. One evening, we discovered that a porcupine had consumed part of one of our tires. In the uninhabited wild, the porcupine feeds on spruce bark, birch, leaves, buds, and aquatic vegetation.

Porcupine quills are hollow and needlelike. They become easily barbed in the mouths and noses of attacking and inexperienced wolves, wolverines, coyotes, and other carnivores. When we are camping in the woods, my husky now spends her nights at the foot of my bed, upon pain of further extractions.

My son once crawled about fifteen feet into a crevice between two housesize rocks deposited by a receding Ice Age glacier. When I asked him to describe what he had found, he said, "I flashed my light around. It was like a cave under the rocks, and from the smell, I think porcupines have been living there for about three thousand years."

To avoid the hardships of northern winters, some animals take to dens. Some grow fur, while others put on blubber. And some animals desert the scene altogether by migrating south. But the common raven is an exception. He can be seen flying on the coldest of days. Unlike the great horned owl, whose soft feathers muffle his passage and make him the master of silent flight, the raven is a noisy bird. Because he eats carrion, it does not matter if his stiff-feathered wings saw away at the dry, cold air. He need not hide. The raven calls, "Walk, walk, walk," in a hollow voice, and at forty or fifty degrees below zero, humans take his advice. They forego their snow machines in order to keep their circulation going. The raven is as black as his kin, the crow, who lives only as far north as Southcentral Alaska, and he has a spade-shaped tail for easy identification in the field. His large nests are built in trees or on cliffs in treeless country. Ravens are considered to be quite intelligent and have been seen dropping or passing a stick or stone among themselves, performing dazzling, aerobatic displays as they fly.

The raven has had a place in cultures as diverse as that of the Norseman and the Eskimo. He has figured as creator of the world in the religious beliefs of the Tlingit, Haida, and other Pacific Northwest Indian tribes. Totem poles bear the bird's image, as do the striking ceremonial robes worn by the tribes. The raven also appears in the multicultural art of modern-day Alaska.

Another bird that is a year-round resident of Alaska is the American dipper. It is also known by its nickname, the water ouzel (OO-zuhl). In the winter of 1959, my husband introduced me to this singular gray bird who lives near the water. Anaktuvuk natives from the Brooks Range call it "Old Woman Sunk," and I learned why as we came upon it. The bird marched right into an unfrozen stream. As if that were not rigorous enough, the water ouzel went under the surface, looking for an insect or a fish egg or two. When it came out, it shook the water from its feathers and then went back for more!

Another bird, the golden-crowned sparrow, returns from the south each spring bringing with him his distinctive song. It is a clear, loud, three-pitched tune that often sounds like "sol-mi-do." Upon hearing the bird's song, a friend was prompted to call the bird a Schubert sparrow, singer of the Unfinished Symphony.

Everyone knows that cats eat birds, but the big, beautiful, tan-gray cat of the northern woods, the short-tailed *Lynx canadensis*, much prefers the snowshoe hare. These "rabbits," as they are called, thrive on low growth vegetation and favor dense cover. Their long, furred hind feet enable them to make tracks in more ways than one, and this is part of what sometimes protects them from the lynx. They also change color from brown and white in summer to their winter pelage of white with black-tipped ears. These advantages are in precarious balance with the large paws and greater strength of the lynx. Every eight or ten years, snowshoe hares build up to as many as sixteen hundred per square mile. The woods appear to be alive with hopping white snowballs. Reasons for an ensuing sudden dropoff in the hare population, followed by a sharp down-swing in the lynx population, are not well understood. It may be that the bark of juvenile birch trees, which is studded with small glands of a toxic material that browsing animals avoid, has something to do with this. This is being studied in several places, including the University of Alaska in Fairbanks.

ON THE EDGE

Near the coastline and as a border between habitat types, brushy thickets grow profusely. Waist-high willow on gravel bars of a braided river bottom is easy going. Tougher to negotiate is thick, second-growth birch. But ask any Alaskan, "What's the worst hiking country?" and he will answer, "Muskeg, which is hummocky bogland. On second thought, however, alders on a hillside are the worst." Alders tangle the feet; they cause all sorts of pratfalls and so are greatly unloved trees. They grow out before they grow up and are avoided by human prowlers.

But alders present no problem to bears. They make their slightly pigeon-toed way along trails they have punched through the alders, leaving paw prints eight inches wide as evidence. A human walking the same paths would have to do so at a crouch. The big bruins have even been seen trampling on the criss-crossed confusion of leaves and curving branches. But this is not so difficult when one is a thirteen hundred-pound powerhouse.

Brown bears go where they will. A friend from Yakutat reported seeing one taking a shortcut across a bay; it was swimming easily a mile from shore. They also eat what they will. According to a sixty-year resident of Kodiak Island, brown bears "are starting to lie in wait" along the trails of transplanted deer. After hunting deer on Uganik Island, my son said that when another hunter fired his rifle, "a good-sized, chocolate bear lifted up his head and moved at a pretty good clip *toward* the sound," in expectation of offal.

Bears on Kodiak and nearby Afognak, are designated *Ursus arctos middendorffi*, a subspecies separated from other brown and grizzly bears by skull characteristics. Coastal bears are usually referred to by laymen as brown, while inland ones are called grizzlies. Largest of the terrestrial bears, brown bears roam the better part of Alaska, sometimes in the forests of the black bears. But they also take to grasslands, open tundra, and timberline and alpine terrain.

Occasionally they take to people, too. One unlucky man was once mauled by a sow with two cubs. Whenever he walked the woods after that, he always carried a dishpan and pounded it with a stick. Another man whose skull was cracked in a bear attack wears a metal plate under his scalp as a reminder. A third fellow, a guide, shot a bear that charged him while he was skinning a client's brownie. The guide hollered, "Shoot!" when he saw the animal bearing down on him, but the client had disappeared into the thin mountain air. Fortunately the guide reached his own rifle in time; the bear fell nine paces from his feet.

If Alaska's state flower is the forget-me-not, and its bird the willow ptarmigan, then surely the state story should be the bear. Stretched or not, such tales make up a large part of Alaskan lore.

Hank Swiss was a trapper and salmon fisherman who lived on the bank of a salmon creek on Cook Inlet's western shore. He put in a garden about three hundred yards from his cabin. For fertilizer Hank filled a garbage can with pink salmon, stuck a cover on it, and let it ripen in the sun. Down a trail, along the creek, came a hungry brown bear. What a windfall! He slurped down the fish and wallowed in the juice. Hank described the bear as "the one we won't have to *look* for."

In brown bear country, can one count on the sanctuary of a tree if things get touchy? For years, people have known that they could not outrun a bear, but they believed that if one climbed speedily beyond reach, a brown bear, with his flat claws, could not catch them. Another myth has been exploded. An experienced woodsman and guide told me how he and a friend tried to keep a brown bear from getting their deer meat for three nights running. First they tied the meat to a branch of a cottonwood tree. The bear climbed up the tree and got to it. The next evening the men suspended it from a tree limb; the bruin again ascended the trunk, crawled out on the seven-inch limb, easily severed it, and had another meal of meat. Trying now to salvage some of their winter grub, the hunters suspended the meat again, but this time they tied

The bright shield of the king eider, *Somateria spectabilis*, loses its high color late in summer.

High rocky slopes and alpine meadows are the habitat of *Lagopus leucurus,* the white-tailed ptarmigan.

the end of the branch to the limb of another tree on the hillside, so the meat would swing away from the marauding bear. They lost again. "The bark was mighty shredded, but he got it." "How far up was it?" I asked. "Thirty-five feet," he answered.

A sow is about half the weight of a boar and is sexually mature at three and a half to four and a half years of age. She is bred in spring or early summer, and on Kodiak, usually dens in the brush and alder zone in November. Excavations are most often on sloping ground where soil is stable and well drained. Usually, two or three cubs are born in the den. They do not look much like their parents, because they weigh less than a pound and have no hair.

From a valley floor on the Alaska Peninsula, my husband was fortunate to watch a sow emerge from her den. The dearth of tracks in the springtime snow indicated to him that she had come out no more than half an hour before he spotted her. The sow sat in front of the entrance for about thirty minutes "like a dog, with her front legs between her knees." Then she wandered off about twenty yards, sat down again, and looked around in a vague manner. She glanced back at the den and finally returned to it, hesitating at first and then pushing her way in. The next day when he saw her, she was more alert. This time, a cub's head poked out from the entrance. Soon it and another cub came out to play and tumble in the snow. They had none of the dopey behavior of the sow, having been awake for two or three months. By the third day, another cub came out. One day later, tracks led away from the site. Then a high wind came up and sealed the entrance.

In the springtime, the essential habitat for bears such as these is along undisturbed beaches. They also frequent south-facing slopes where green plants begin to grow after the snow melts. Bears are lured to the sand strips and rocks to feed on kelp or winter kills of deer or elk. On occasion they may find a beached whale or seal. The big bears also eat skunk cabbage, cow parsnip, and sea lovage. These last two are wild celeries that are edible by humans. Bears graze on false hellebore; sedges; grasses; lupine; and a curious tough, cone-like plant, red poque, that grows as a parasite on the roots of the alder.

In summer these coastal bears feed heavily on salmon. This high intake of protein accounts for the body size of brown bears. Standing boars measure ten feet, much taller than inland grizzlies. A biologist in Yakutat reported that the preferred diet of the local bears was salmon and wild strawberries, not a bad choice for four- or two-legged creatures.

Radio-tracking efforts by the United States Fish and Wildlife Service have produced an estimate of about one bear per four square miles on Kodiak. When the fish are running, however, concentrations of bear along the streams are much higher. A woman whose family fishes salmon commercially on such a beach reported seeing an average of eight bears a day last summer. Her children are taught to ride their three-wheelers near the water's edge in order to keep an eye on the trees.

My first two summers in Alaska were spent on a beach well-traveled by the bears. One morning we left a load of fish in our open dory. As the tide ran out, a bear ambled down the mud flat, climbed in the dory, and helped himself. Even more frustrating to us were the times when the bears picked the nets. They would grab a fish and begin walking away with it, tearing the nets as they went. A two hour mending job would lie ahead of me. We tried putting smudge pots at the end of each net, but the bears ignored the warning. The scariest times were when we patrolled the beaches at night. That is when we talked to ourselves *loudly*; that is when we indulged in an inordinate amount of bad singing.

But from a safe distance, the bears were fun to watch: guzzling a seal smelly enough to keep us a quarter of a mile upwind; stripping plump huckleberries from the bushes; sliding and somersaulting down a grassy slope.

One morning we spied a sow and two cubs meandering up the beach toward our fish shack. The cubs were in the lead, playing and paying scant attention to what lay ahead. Suddenly the sow caught our scent, stood on her rear feet, and woofed. The cubs turned to her. She began to walk backwards, appearing at each step to beckon the cubs by alternately waving front paws in front of her chest. She let out another woof, and they sped back to her. When she dropped to all fours, they bounded off and took to the thick undergrowth.

Bears live in stories as surely as in the bush. A Tlingit myth that was recorded at the turn of the century provided an explanation for the tradition of painting a cross on a slain bear. A member of the Raven Clan, in deep grief over the loss of his wife, his child, and all of his property, decided he wanted to be done with life. Unwilling to kill himself, he lay down on a nearby bear trail, hoping that the bears would do it for him. Soon they came, led by an old silvertip boar. The man became fainthearted and so told the bears he had a feast planned for them the next day. "But if you are going to kill me," he said, "I'm willing to die. I've lost all my family and my property." The large bear turned and instructed the other bears in a whine, and they all retreated to the woods. The man went home and prepared for the feast. He cleaned his house by scattering fresh sand about his cooking area. He gathered dry wood, and he painted his upper arms and chest with crosses and stripes. The others in the village cringed with fright and would have nothing to do with the planned festivities.

When the bears came the next morning, the man served them cranberries preserved in grease. The large old bear then turned to the man and spoke in his whine for many minutes, but the man could not understand what he was saying. As the bears filed out of the house, they licked the stripes from the man's arms and chest in a gesture of thanks.

The following day, the smallest bear of the troop came back. But he appeared to his host in the form of a young man. He explained that he had been captured and adopted by the bears. He asked the man if he had been able to decipher the old bear's story. "No," said the sad man. The young bear explained, "He said he had heard of you before we saw you lying in the forest trail. He told you to think of him when you are grieving for your own lost family, because he is also desolate. The same happened to him, and he has lost all his friends, too."

Forever after, any bear killed by the Tlingits was honored by having a cross painted on its skin. And if a feast was to be held, not only friends, but any enemies camped nearby were invited to it.

Tales such as this one helped to pass long winter nights in the old days. One need only turn one's back on the world of electricity and television to recapture such times. When snow is flying, candles are snuffed, and sleeping bags have been pulled tight around the shoulders, bear yarns can weave people together.

TRANSPLANTS AND INTRODUCTIONS

The Alaska Department of Fish and Game determined that the country near where I sang with the wolves was fit to accommodate Alaska's third transplant of American bison. The buffalo, as it is popularly called, is massive, especially at its forequarters. Its large head carries a pair of short, upward-curving horns.

We were often alerted by our children when the buffalo were approaching. The kids would be looking out the windows past their correspondence school lessons, and they would spot the dark buffalo adults and lighter calves as they crossed the frozen lake. Even though the cows weighed more than a thousand pounds and the bulls up to a ton, there was no need to fear that the buffalo would fall through the ice. The temperatures in that part of the country bottomed out the thermometer at sixty-four degrees below zero. It might have been even colder; we could not tell. The ice on the lake was forty-eight inches thick and strong enough to hold a plane loaded with supplies. The bison withstood such cold well and traveled the ice every few days.

Having bison around us put me in a historical mood one day, and I decided to burn some buffalo "chips," as the Plains Indians and the sodbuster's wife had done before me. I will stick to spruce wood; the odor of the chips was cloying, reminiscent of incense left over from the sixties.

The first bison were transplanted in Delta Junction. The herd's problems in subsequent years made wildlife managers take a second look at mixing cropland and wildlife, combining domestic species and wild animals, and introducing outsiders, or exotics, into country new to them.

The Delta herd had done well since it was first introduced in 1928. After Alaska gained statehood, barley crops were added to the region as part of a plan to foster farming in the forty-ninth state. But conflicts developed as the bison turned from grazing on the wild grasses and sedges of the winter range to eating cultivated fields which they evidently preferred. As a result, grains are now planted in areas far from the farmers' fields to entice the buffalo away from settled areas.

The introduction of reindeer and cattle has also created conflicts. In western Alaska, reindeer (descended from caribou domesticated in Europe centuries ago) simply take to the trail with their wild cousins when given the chance. If isolated by fences or herded onto peninsulas, they do better. Cattle ranchers have had to shoot bears and other carnivores who prey on their free-ranging stock. With that in mind, biologists have strongly recommended against the practice of running livestock on unpenned public land in Alaska. They also fear that domestic sheep diseases would be readily passed on to the wild and majestic Dall sheep, which are found only in Alaska and a corner of Canada.

The relocation of musk-oxen has been successful. Once a wild species here, it was exterminated, probably by overhunting. The long-haired animals were brought back to the Alaska Territory in 1930 and were soon transplanted to Nunivak Island. Other herds have been established elsewhere. Some are kept in domesticated groups, while others are in the wild. The musk-ox differs from the bison in the long downsweep of its horns, which it uses with brute force in rutting combat. Musk-oxen also have much longer capes of hair than buffalo. A wooly underlayer is shed in the spring.

Collected by Eskimos, it is spun into a yarn called qiviut. Handsome caps and other knitted and woven goods are made from it. Like bison, elk, and a few other species, musk-oxen can be hunted in Alaska by permit only.

Relocating native species is not without its problems. In 1967, it was noted that the ground-nesting Aleutian Canada goose had been decimated by Arctic foxes. These foxes had been transported from farther north in Alaska by Russian and American fur traders in the period from 1836-1930. The foxes had been let loose on the islands and were trapped whenever their numbers warranted. During the Great Depression, prices dropped in the fur market, and the fur-trading business was largely abandoned. The fox population began to increase rapidly, and the bird population continued to be their prey. It is likely that some geese survived only because two of the islands had such poor harbors that the early fur traders were prevented from putting foxes there.

Once the geese were given endangered species status, recovery programs were initiated. Hunting was stopped on their wintering grounds in California and Oregon. On small islands in the Aleutian chain that could be covered on foot, foxes were trapped or shot. Kiska, an island occupied by the Japanese in 1942, was considered too large for these methods. The Fish and Wildlife Service decided to apply to the Environmental Protection Agency for permission to use poison on the estimated seven hundred foxes. Other wildlife at risk from the poisoning were a few eagles, ravens, and gulls who were potential scavengers of the fox carcasses. But any loss of birds was expected to be renewed from resident or adjacent populations. Many Alaskans had no quarrel with the plan, although some did not like the use of poison. Poisoning brought to mind the indiscriminate days of wolf-poisoning. In time, most people came around, including the members of some moderate environmental groups. One group took the position that, in order to save a species from extinction, the eradication of interloping individuals from healthy populations was justified.

The EPA granted the permit, and the plan was implemented. At first count, six Aleutian Canada geese had returned to Kiska; four gulls and most of the foxes, if not all, had died. The island's bird population continues to be monitored. Any surviving foxes will be killed. The Fish and Wildlife Service may apply for the use of poison on other islands, but the islands will be chosen carefully. Kiska has no native land mammals and no human population, conditions that are hard to find elsewhere.

Another fowl, the dusky Canada goose, faces an uncertain future. In the giant Good Friday earthquake of 1964, the Copper River Delta was raised by six feet. Dusky Canada goose nests, which previously were subject to occasional tidal flooding but were more often protected by water from prowling bears and coyotes, were also raised. For about ten years the geese prospered. But new plant and brush growth and drier walking attracted predators to the area. They began to prey heavily on the geese. Glaucous gulls, whose numbers had also increased when the land rose, joined in by taking goose eggs. To the south, hunters from Oregon and Washington shot some for the table. So did farmers, perturbed at crop depredations by Vancouver Canada geese which mixed with the declining dusky geese.

In the last seven years, observers have seen the numbers of dusky Canada goose drop from twenty-five thousand to twelve

In the fall, the first indication of a bull moose, *Alces alces,* is often a flash of antlers.

Some areas of Alaska have as many as five nests of Arctic loons, *Gavia arctica*, per square mile.

thousand. To prevent a further decrease, officials of the Alaska Department of Fish and Game and members of the public have come up with a list of options. One plan calls for transplanting the dusky Canada goose far out in the Gulf of Alaska to Middleton, a flyspeck of an island which has no major predators.

Transplants are not a one-way street: goats taken from Alaska now live in the state of Oregon, and Alaskan eagles fly in the skies of New York's Adirondack Mountains.

TAKING THE LONG VIEW

The words "*Rangifer tarandus*" roll off the tongue like an incantation. Their meaning lies far back in time; the first name evokes great expanses traversed, while the second may refer to the tundra or nomad. I have wondered if *tarandus* stems from the fabled and prehistoric country of Turan, which lay between the Soviet Union and Afghanistan and was said to have been peopled by nomads who pre-dated the Aryans in Asia and Europe.

Rangifer tarandus, the caribou, are famous nomads. In North America, the Algonquian called the animal "pawer" or "scratcher." We call it the Barren Ground caribou, a fitting name for the stretches of tundra west and east of Hudson's Bay where it lives.

Caribou have a mystique shared by few land animals here in the north. Surely this has to do with human perceptions of freedom and wilderness, which the animal symbolizes. Is the mystique justified? One must first examine the animal's habitat.

High-powered lenses bring the caribou into focus, but then his setting may become a blur. To see the animal properly, one must get a feel for the tundra. The term most often associated with tundra is treeless. Tundra can be flat and wet and stretch for hundreds of miles. Or it can be dry and can climb the slopes of an inland mountain. It can also range along low hills. North of the Brooks Range, the tundra is characterized by poor drainage and underlying permafrost; in the Aleutians, it may be an early plant successional stage, much prolonged, where trees have not yet gained a foothold from the last Ice Age; in the mountains, it is controlled by elevation. In some spots, the tundra is a sponge of cream-colored moss, a mat of tiny plants, set in a flock of puddles and ponds. Thousands of caribou and millions of birds, insects, and lemmings are active there in summer. In the western and northern tundra, the Arctic fox hunts for ground squirrels, voles, and birds in his warm-weather fur of brown and yellow-white. He also eats berries and raids nests. When his prey flies south or goes to ground, the fox changes to a winter coat of pure white to camouflage his forays in the snow. The foxes of the far northern coasts follow polar bears and eat from their seal kills on the ice pack. A phase of permanent dark brown or charcoal lives on the Aleutians and Pribilofs.

One of the world's most thinly populated regions is the vast, northwest Arctic coast, a region the size of New England, New York, New Jersey, and half of Pennsylvania combined. Its population density equals but *one* of their smallest towns. That gives an idea of the area and human population density of the western Arctic. There, *R. tarandus* outnumber humans thirty to one.

Alaska has about twenty caribou herds. A herd is defined as animals who calve each year on historic grounds distinct from other caribou. The caribou migrate to these grounds each spring, a movement thought to be triggered by changes in light and assessments of snow depth and crust quality. Calving grounds are used by cows and yearlings. Normally each cow gives birth to one calf. Adult bulls stay late on the wintering ground common to both sexes. The herd merges again on the summer range. The bigger the herd, the greater the need for forage, hence, for some, an extensive range is necessary.

One of Alaska's caribou herds is small and static. It is a transplanted group that calves about a mile from the end of the Kenai runway, where jets, helicopters, and many small private planes operate daily. The caribou are harassed not by wolves and bears, but by the town dogs. This herd is not expected to grow much because of its limited range, but it provides many people with their only glimpse of caribou.

When I am out picking wild greens in the mountain tundra in June, I feel a curious bond with the caribou. We both eat dwarf fireweed, arctic dock, and roseroot, a sedum plant. But caribou also browse on sedges, grasses, willow stems, catkins, buds, and leaves. They eat dwarf shrubs such as blueberry and birch and other flowering plants such as the unusual white gentian. Their winter staple is the lichen, a plant that may take fifty to one hundred years to grow.

Because of its long life, relationship of the lichen to atomic fallout and the Arctic food chain has been the basis for some northern studies. Prior to the 1962 Nuclear Test Ban Treaty between the United States and the Soviet Union, radioactive isotopes, products of fission, were introduced to the atmosphere. Strontium 90 and cesium 137, two of these isotopes, act like calcium and potassium and are taken up by plants. The short-lived leaves and berries of deciduous plants die within a year, but in lichens, the elements remain. Since strontium 90 collects in bone, and cesium 137 in skeletal muscles, a wolf that eats both bone and flesh of a lichen-fed caribou is also ingesting both isotopes. Man, mainly a flesh-eater, takes in only one. Tests performed on Eskimos in peak fallout years of the late 1960s showed an increase in the elements one or two months following ingestion of winter caribou. Eskimos received dietary radiation levels that were about ten percent higher than normal, but less than one would have received from atmospheric radiation in Denver, for instance, because of its higher elevation. The concentrations of radiation were highest in wolves. Differences were noted between wolves that ate lichen-fed caribou and moose that ate deciduous growth. Fallout from the Chernobyl nuclear accident of 1986 was minimal in Alaska in comparison to the years following atmospheric testing. But many nuclear power plants are operating in Europe and Asia, and the winds blow on. Alaska still has radioactive lichens, and they are still being consumed. It is a haunting reminder of man's past acts.

Such human effects on the caribou belie the myth of their complete freedom. Although it would appear otherwise to the casual eye as the great nomads file from a remote mountain pass or leave parallel trails in the tundra, caribou, like any other animal, are also bound by nature's constraints—the ransom demanded for the gift of life.

One of the constraints is placed upon them by the combination of weather and the ancient pull on the cows to reach favorable, and so historic, calving grounds.

There, in years of normal weather, newborn calves and their mothers usually are bonded within two hours. Within a few days, nursery herds are formed. In ten days or so, healthy calves are making twenty to thirty miles a day with their herd. In some situations, cows are unable to reach their traditional calving grounds because of storms or snow conditions, and they calve early. The instinct is so strong to reach these areas that, within two days, the herd is again afoot, leaving many calves behind to die.

Neither are caribou free from the pests of daily existence. On still days, swarms of mosquitoes, whose females need blood to nourish their eggs, descend on the big mammals. The caribou are driven to congregate on windy ridges, on ice patches, or even to the sea for relief. Warble flies also plague caribou, depositing their eggs on the skin. Their larvae burrow into and migrate under the skin to emerge later. Bot flies seem to put the caribou into a state of frenzy; buzzing like bumblebees, they wriggle up their noses. This sets them running wild. One of the reasons for the greater body size of caribou in the Adak Island herd is the lack of biting insects.

Caribou are graceful and a pleasure to watch. We have seen them nap in the sunshine, get up, and with one foot asleep, shake it, and hobble off. Young ones are curious. They have come close to us, circled around us, and walked on. They appear to go slowly, but they cover twice our ground in the same amount of time. During calving days, field biologists must be cautious; a newborn caribou will bond to anything alive, even the scientific type.

What will be the future of these young caribou? In coming years, politics and industry will play an important role. Factionalism regarding state wildlife matters is not new. Much of it centers on the caribou and oil development. The Trans-Alaska Pipeline which carries crude oil from the Arctic Coast to Valdez, is a case in point. One side contends that cows and calves avoid the new pipeline-road area; another counters by saying they previously avoided river bottom sites like the present corridor because of brushy cover fit for wolves and bears. A third faction notes, "What's the difference when the herd is, in fact, increasing?" A fourth says the jury is still out on the controversy. Whenever new biological findings are made public, it seems that each faction interprets the results to fit their preexisting philosophy.

Battles continue over the use of wild areas such as the Arctic National Wildlife Refuge. At the northernmost part of Alaska, the Porcupine Caribou Herd calves and crosses over into Canada for part of the year. "How many caribou are enough?" The answers mean the most to the ones not talking—the caribou themselves.

Caribou and wolves are so intertwined in the life and lore of the far north, it is easy to forget that the latter prosper in southern forests, too. There they mainly prey on deer, moose, beaver, and fish. The wolves of the south are darker and smaller than the gray wolves of the northern tundra but litters of varied color tones are born throughout the state.

"The big, bad wolf," "the wolf at the door," and "a wolf in sheep's clothing" are age-old phrases that derive from hard times, superstitious times, and times of actual depredation. Perhaps, as psychologists suggest, folk tales such as Little Red Riding Hood and the wolf evolved as a way of putting fears into manageable form. If so, stories about wolves may stem from Medieval days, when starvation and disease were common and wolves lived outside the town gates. These stories may even echo an older tale of mankind's

earliest memories, when wolf eyes glinted from beyond a circle of fire. In our own time, we see that precious stock is still lost to wolves, coyotes, foxes, and eagles.

But we have learned to know the wolf better and suspect him less. We recognize that wolves live in an intricate pack relationship; each sex has its own hierarchy which is based on dominance. They breed in March, living in a den dug deeply into a bank or hillside, and bear an average of five pups per litter in May. Young wolves, like kit foxes and bear cubs, are engaging creatures. However, their rough and tumble play is not all fun and games; it prepares them for their role as hunter.

Alaskan wolves have had a checkered history. Older people who live on the rivers of the Interior have passed on beliefs that link the wolf with the beginning of the world. Their stories tell of the power of the animal's spirit. Some Athabascan Indians still adhere to taboos against women's and children's proximity to skins and carcasses. They believe that methods of trapping and hunting the wolf may determine one's future luck in those activities. By midcentury, wolves were being poisoned by federal personnel, but that practice has been discontinued. Aerial shooting of wolves by the Alaska Department of Fish and Game in order to increase the ungulate prey for human needs is a hotly contested issue at present. On the one hand, state wildlife managers have proved they can increase caribou calf production from fifteen percent to twenty percent by restricting wolf numbers. For every fifty thousand caribou, that would mean twenty-five hundred more calves. On the other hand, critics advocate a more primitive balance of wolf and caribou. They would prefer to restrict human hunting. Some would like to close it down altogether. Hunters have asked to be included in the airplane hunts, but only department personnel may do so now and only in certain areas. Few would like to see the wolf gone, though. We all realize its beauty and its place in the natural world. We are all singers at heart.

AT A MOUNTAIN POND

I've walked the high country,
Where a blueberry carpet runs a hundred miles long.

Alaskan song

Part of the year I live at a pond near timberline in the Alaska Range. The pond lies in a basin below a hill where a few spruces have been so blown by the winds, they have the layered look of an Oriental print. The short wiry bushes at my feet are *Rhododendron lapponicum*, the smallest member of a genus that grows throughout the world. Its blossoms resemble a tiny azalea. Here also are dwarf birch, crowberries, cranberries, blueberries, club mosses, sphagnum, grass, and sedge. Yellow arnica and a white parrya flower grow in the short brush. On a rock slide across the pond, I find an alp lily and *Calypso bulbosa*, or fairy slipper. I pick the latter before learning that its presence is rare here.

A balsam poplar grove hides in the lee of the hill. Willows and alders edge a streambed and stud an old beaver dam. There a willow ptarmigan tunelessly clucks his "buk-buk-bukbukbukbuk" call. The red patches over his eyes identify him as a male to me and to a female that dips under a spruce at my approach. In spring, both are mottled brown and white.

Mountain ridges and alpine meadows are the haunts of Dall ewes.

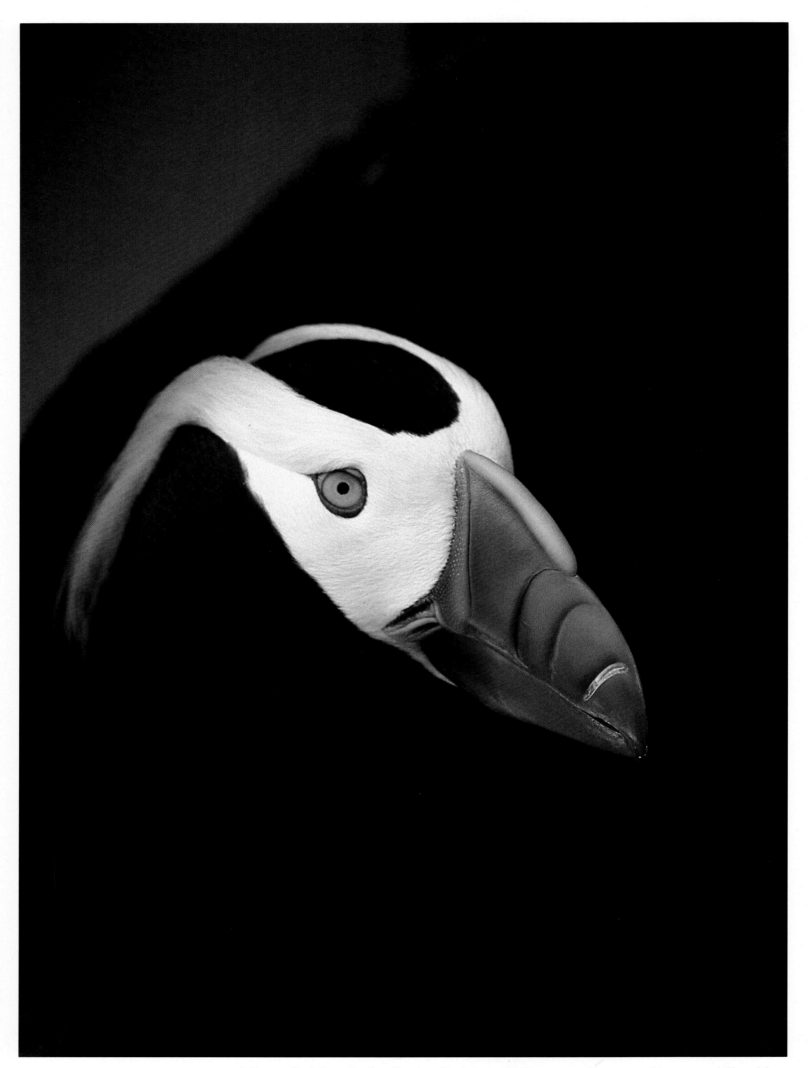

Sailors called the tufted puffin, *Lunda cirrhata*, the "sea parrot" because of its orange bill and feet.

It is June. At one end of the pond, tall grass flourishes in the water, and a green-headed duck paddles from it. The duck is followed by a dull-looking one and five miniature ones. Are they mallards? I thought drakes shed their bright feathers after mating and looked like hens while they were temporarily flightless. Could these be greater scaups this far inland? They cannot be northern shovelers, whose broad bills would give them away, even at this distance. I have forgotten my binoculars, and the bird book lies on the table. But I do recognize a lesser yellowlegs who swoops over the marsh, trying to distract me. They say he swims, which is unusual for a shore bird, but I have not seen him do this yet. There is another duck, a pintail, who is feeding and waggling his feet in the air like an afterthought.

At the other end of the pond, I see a pile of tiny freshwater snail shells awash in the cup of a moose print. This is where a cow and young bull showed up last night to drink.

One spring we saw several Dall rams feeding on the slopes above our camp. We spotted them three days in a row, but the night before a wild windstorm blew in, they moved out. Specialists say there is no prestorm behavior in mountain sheep, although some marine mammals practice it; they are thought to be responding to atmospheric pressure changes.

One year, when we put up a small shelter, the Arctic ground squirrels burrowed up inside it during the winter, throwing humps of dirt against the walls. They are welcome visitors, especially for the dog. He is taunted by their whistles and vainly tries to catch them before they take to their tunnels.

I have never seen any marmots here or at the base of the rock slide nearby where I would expect to find them. Perhaps this region is beyond their western limit. When marmots stand up in late summer, they look like fat pears from months of easy feeding; in the winter they will go into true hibernation. Hoary marmots den alone, but the Alaska marmot of the most northerly ranges does so in colonies, sealing entrances to the burrow with a mixture of feces and vegetation.

I have looked in vain here for the collared pika, a tiny mammal nicknamed "rock rabbit." It is a member of the hare family and lives in colonies in alpine rock piles. Unlike the marmot and the ground squirrel, it does not hibernate. Instead, it lives off the stockpiles it has accumulated in summer and early fall. Food gathering is done at breakneck speed. The vegetation is stacked and turned near the entrance to the pika's abode. After it has dried in the sun, it is stored under rocks.

These small mammals are often hidden and always elusive. But the grizzly bear, who comes sniffing around my shelter and leaves claw marks on the tarp, has no need to hide from the little animals—or from me. In fact, I hide from him, even though I always carry a rifle in bear country in the event of a charge.

Grizzlies spend more time than black bears in sub-Alpine and Alpine habitat. They also den higher, sometimes in rock caves. These bears of inland Alaska feed primarily on vegetation. On the river bar below the pond, I can see holes where they have dug bear root. They eat other green growth, carrion, insect larvae, and berries. Ground squirrels and the young of ungulates make an occasional meal. Several years ago, it was suggested that grizzlies were killing a good number of moose calves along the Denali Highway. As an experiment, some of the bears were tranquilized and removed by airplane. The moose calf survival rate climbed, given that edge of the first six weeks of life, free of predation. Most of the bears eventually returned, though, some from as far as 175 miles away! But bear-lifts are impractical, even if they are exciting. As a result, the Alaska Department of Fish and Game liberalized the hunting season there on bears. The moose population has picked up, and the study goes on to see if other factors, such as mild winters, are also at work.

Camping with bears may appeal to some, but it pays to keep a clean tent site. An acquaintance was reminded of this when her daughter's head was sniffed and gently prodded by a grizzly from outside the thin nylon membrane so generously called a tent "wall." Had fresh meat been in the tent, the bear might have been more than just curious.

The pond in winter reflects a different tale. Tracks on the ice tell of a fox padding across the snow, but they say nothing about its color. Could it have been that flamboyant fellow, the red fox? Or was it a darker cross fox, with its mixed fur of brown, red and gold? Might it have been a prize silver fox, with its luxurious black fur tipped in gray?

More recent paw prints appear to have been made by a coyote. The tracks lead down a small draw along the pond's outlet. Despite the cold, the creek is open in spots. A river otter has been here, too, trotting and gliding along, and the fox has stopped to sniff its trail. The otter frolicked on the bank, for I can see his snowslide to the water. I have seen the otter take to the slide time after time like a single-minded child on a school playground.

Occasionally a wolverine goes by. Today I find only a very old set of tracks, filled with blown snow and rounded on the edges. Few are seen in the wild. I have seen the tail end of one bounding around a curve on the trail ahead of me. But I will probably walk many a mile on snowshoes before meeting up with the other end. The wolverine is as solitary in his habits as the trapper who tries to outwit him. Fur trapping makes up a large part of the incomes of some Alaskans. Wolverine fur is highly valued for use in parka ruffs; breath does not readily freeze on it. The animals are tough but protective of their young. Sometimes they steal bait and fur from traps and they are messy when breaking and entering human habitation. But to call them vindictive and vicious is an overreaction. They need only be called wolverines.

Moose, caribou, and wolves are rarely seen here in winter, preferring the more heavily timbered country down-river. That is good fortune for the newest tenants of the pond, *Castor canadensis*, the beaver, who came here three years after I did. They took over an abandoned beaver house and began to stake out "musk piles" flanking it. Then they started flooding the pond. After repairing the old dam, the beaver began another about twenty feet in front of it, right in the spot I had been planning to build a rustic bridge. By their second year, two newer dams had been built below that, and one of my trails was under a few feet of water. Water now extended well past the ptarmigan's old territory. The pond had flooded the duck grass, and big rocks, which served as perches, were covered. I wondered how all this would affect the birds who usually summer here. My wooden boundary stakes were awash on the shoreline; perhaps the beavers were trying to cover *my* "musk piles." I expect to see them strengthening the lodge or the dam someday soon.

I hope the beaver can keep their dams in order. They need about two or three feet of free water beneath the ice to be able to swim along underground tunnels from house to feed pile. The feed pile is located in the lake bottom close by. Filled with poplar and willows assiduously gathered in the summer, the pile must last until the ice melts.

Did the last beaver freeze out? Or did they eat themselves out of feed in this montane border habitat? The house they built was free from the ravages of predation; no gaping holes indicated that a bear or wolverine or wolf had taken a meal. Nor have there been beaver trappers in this country. Perhaps I will see the full cycle of the beaver. My own cycle seems to be overlapping theirs and that of the fox, the ducks, and the tiny rhododendron. More intersections are here than those simply found on trails.

SEPARATING THE SHEEP FROM THE GOATS

From high alpine meadows and bastions of rock, perhaps Dall sheep observe the cycles of life below. An estimated seventy thousand sheep live in the forty-ninth state, most of them in mountainous habitat. Both Dall sheep and mountain goats use cliffs and peaks as escape or avoidance terrain. Seldom is it easy for predators to penetrate their domain.

No goats overlook our mountain camp in the Interior, but this is typical country for sheep. They live in an area that extends from the Kenai and Wrangell mountains north to the Brooks Range. Goats thrive in the highest southeastern coastal ranges, where precipitation is stored as snow and glacial ice. Their range overlaps the sheep's only in the latter's southerly portion.

To say that goats prefer a wet habitat to the dry lands of the sheep may be an oversimplification. Goats can tolerate deeper snow than sheep. They routinely cross ice fields that are five miles long. Because of their heavily insulating, wooly hair, grown thick even in summer, goats are at home among the snow banks and glaciers of the coastal ranges. A biologist reported that he once lost track of the goats' radio-collar signals when he was conducting a survey by airplane. He tried a second pass at a lower altitude and finally caught sight of the bottom of their legs under a glacier's lip. They appeared to be simply taking a cooler. This biologist thinks the goats are tied to the southern regions by these permanent ice fields.

Goats and sheep differ in many other ways. In winter, goats can eat hemlock, alder, and fern roots, whereas sheep are limited to the grass and sedge stems they find on windy ridges or in shallow snow. Sheep move in a more flowing, fluid manner than goats, whose movements are often described as "deliberate." The goat has heavy shoulder muscles and specialized hooves. His hooves have a wide spread, enabling him to almost "grasp" a small rock pinnacle and pull himself up. Goats have been seen climbing nearly perpendicular glacier sides, perhaps by using footholds unseen by human observers.

Socially, sheep differ radically from goats. Rams are dominant, butting other rams and females about. Among goats, nannies usually pick on billies, and they both pick on kids.

Future rational development in the state makes paramount the setting aside of critical habitat. Northern scientists found that although sheep show great fidelity to their home ranges, they traveled twelve miles each spring to visit a favorite mineral lick.

Why? It was thought that a desire and need for sodium dictated this move. Researchers now suggest that the need to ingest calcium and magnesium is what attracts the sheep. These minerals help to balance the sheep's intake of potassium from plants. A noted sheep authority thinks that attendance at the lick may depend on plant moisture. In dry years, plants take up less potassium, and, it appears, fewer sheep come to the lick. This information, if fully documented, will help game officials. We would not think of moving a fish from water to land and expect him to survive. Nor would we put him in a bowl of chicken soup. Sheep and other animals not only need licks, but, it seems, they need the correct kinds of licks, and they may require them more in some years than in others. Should a new road be built on such a site? Should such a spot be flooded?

Sheep and goat hunting are popular activities in Alaska. Goat horns are small, but the challenge of hunting a goat in its taxing habitat makes it a trophy animal. Dall rams possess a magnificent set of horns which reach full curl by about seven years of age. If maximum harvest is the desired management goal, some state biologists believe this can be achieved by limiting hunting to full curl rams only. Their numbers will eventually increase. The theory suggests that breeding rams may lose much fat during the rut, leaving themselves open to greater mortality than non-breeding rams in the following winter. If hunting younger rams is made illegal, and if they do not rut because of competition from older rams, more may mature to full curl status. Greater lamb production is also indicated for a herd managed in this way.

Goats living at higher elevations can rest secure for a while. But what about sheep? For all their wilderness mystique, sheep seem able to habituate to man somewhat. They have learned to live close to roads, photographers, aircraft, shooting ranges, and barking dogs. They have even been noticed licking the ditches alongside recently salted roads. But the vast majority of sheep live in fairly remote areas. Displacing them from certain home ranges may be a critical mistake. The *type* of development that is permitted is significant, too. Destroying habitat, in the words of a sheep lover, "is gonna hurt."

ON WIND AND WATER

April 16 - Ducks came back
April 17 - Ducks for dinner
(A note carved on a cabin door frame.)

In Alaska, many birds come and go. But there is a soft spot in Alaskan hearts for our permanent avian residents, who lighten an often dreary winter. In October and November, an extraordinary congregation meets on a stretch of the Chilkat River near Klukwan. This is on the road to coastal Haines. Bald eagles, sometimes numbering up to thirty-five hundred, assemble to feed on the spawned-out salmon. They pepper the gravel bars and roost in trees close to the road.

Immature bald eagles resemble golden eagles but can be identified by their bare lower legs and a leading edge of white wing feathers. There is no mistaking the adult, however, with its white head and its tail that flashes as it cants from side to side in directional flight.

Tusks emerge at age two in both sexes of the Pacific walrus, *Odobenus rosmarus divergens*.

Most brown/grizzly bears, *Ursus arctos*, prefer meat and fish, but some are primarily herbivorous.

The use of the eagle's habitat in the Chilkat River Valley became a source of conflict by 1979. Timber interests, fishermen, local job seekers, a mining firm, natives, conservationists, preservationists, the United States Fish and Wildlife Service, and state agencies all wanted a say. It was a prime example of the kind of scrapping that goes on whenever a proposal is made over the use of a resource or a tract of land in modern Alaska.

The National Audubon Society was alerted by conservationists early in the conflict and played a large part in the compromise solution that was reached. A joint effort by all parties concerned resulted in the creation of the Chilkat Bald Eagle Preserve as critical habitat and the State Forest Resource Management Area nearby. For some, it is an uneasy truce.

On the Chilkat, as elsewhere in the state, the bald eagle consumes fish in normal years. In lean ones, he also feeds on prey common to the golden eagle: small mammals, birds, and waterfowl. A duck hunter in Kachemak Bay reported losing two ducks in a row. Before he could retrieve them, they were snatched by eagles watching from their tree tops.

Golden eagles are ordinarily found on cliffs. They often lay two eggs in an aerie that measures ten feet by four feet. Sometimes only one egg survives. The young eagle grows to a size that almost rivals his famous but distant "bald" kin, who has a wingspan of nearly seven and a half feet. The golden eagles' elegant soaring and wheeling flight against a light sky is a favorite sight among hikers. Champion climbers receive an even greater thrill as they watch the eagles from above.

A tundra nester of note is the jaeger (YEA-gurr), which means "hunter" in German. The jaeger preys on lemmings, voles, small birds, and carrion. It can steal the meal of another bird by terrorizing it into disgorging the food in midair. It is known as a pirate for such actions. Parent jaegers work in concert to feed their young. They will dismember a lemming held in their bills by pulling away from each other. Jaegers, like lynx, are dependent on the availability of cyclical prey. In years when the lemming population is down, jaeger numbers are locally low also.

Many waterfowl summer in Alaska. In the vast nesting ground of the Yukon-Kuskokwim Delta, four species of geese have been dwindling. They are the cackling Canada goose, the Pacific white-fronted goose, the emperor goose, and the Pacific brant. To help convince delta hunters and egg gatherers of the need to restrict the take of these geese, ten village leaders were flown by the government to the geese's wintering grounds in California. Although the leaders were intrigued at seeing where the geese had flown for generations, they were disturbed to see the shrinking acreage available to them. Only small wetland pockets remained among the crowded cities. The leaders agreed to limit hunting and close some areas to hunting and egg-taking.

This account touches on a sensitive and politically charged issue facing Alaskans: the continuing debate on subsistence. The state has recently passed laws that give rural residents the highest priority in the taking of fish and game in the event of a shortage. Many urban users who have come to Alaska expressly to hunt and fish consider it unfair to allocate fishing and hunting rights by geography. They argue that current sport and commercial regulations cover all residents adequately. But in many bush communities, cash income is small. High transportation costs raise the price of groceries to astronomical levels. Subsistence helps in towns like Shishmaref, near the Bering Land Bridge National Monument, where inhabitants live on subsistence fare as varied as bearded seal, whitefish, tom cod, moose, ptarmigan, berries, and greens. In a recent year, residents at Kaktovik, on the Arctic coast, took twenty-five hundred char plus other wild game. Besides this geographical favoritism, regulations have added unsettling racial overtones to wildlife issues. Some federal rules favor hunters and fishermen of Indian, Eskimo, and Aleut extraction, regardless of their income. The web of life in Alaska is tangled indeed.

With more than three hundred eighty species of birds that summer in Alaska, encounters with them are many. A family of gaily blotched harlequin ducks sails by. The female has white head patches, and the male is engagingly striped, spotted, and patched in white, smoky blue, and rust. Both go by the somewhat hysterical name of *Histrionicus histrionicus*, "actor-actor." When approached in early spring, snow buntings rise up in a cloud and blow away en masse. But again it is winter birds one knows best—cheerful black and white chickadees, and reddish grosbeaks who brighten a drab, dark, December day. In a cabin in the bush, one can carry on regular conversations with these old friends.

OVER AND ON AND UNDER THE SEA

A caribou's long line tracks the tundra. A bear trail etches a riverbank. Both are marks of the landlubber. But where is the path of a whale or a million salmon? The sea and air *are* different; passages there go unrecorded. Charts that show avian and marine migration patterns are studded with question marks. There are question marks about a tundra nester, the red-necked phalarope. Its female lays eggs and then leaves incubation and nurturing of the young to her mate. Its nest is built on land, but later it flies to southern oceans in a path unknown. Question marks exist for the Aleutian tern. Where it winters in the North Pacific remains a mystery. There are unanswered questions about salmon, sea otters, and sea lions.

In 1986, one of thirty-four hundred bottles that had been released during 1979 in Alaskan waters was found in Scotland. This provided one answer to questions about ocean drift. State personnel think that many of the bottles tossed overboard in the Bering Sea study drifted north through the strait between Alaska and Siberia. Those not recovered before reaching Point Hope in northwest Alaska probably have been frozen into the ice pack, or they may lie on Soviet and other northern beaches. Will they be returned? Knowledge gained from the bottle study can be applied to the path an oil spill might take. This information may be invaluable in saving the lives and habitat of fish, marine birds, and mammals.

Northern sea waters abound with fish, fowl, crustaceans, and mammals. Man's favorites live here: salmon, halibut, shrimp, and crab. Salmon is presently the great bonanza, accounting for up to $500 million in Alaska's commercial fish revenue each year. In times of declining oil revenues, a fishing dollar spent in Bethel or Anchorage or Ketchikan is warmly welcomed. The fish is also prized as sport or subsistence catch. A fish rack, a smokehouse, a pressure cooker, or a freezer have become basic equipment for many residents. Winter grub for my family includes game meat, wild greens, and berries, but we also freeze and can fish.

Answers about salmon are crucial to many Alaskans. The greatest migrations are undertaken by those creatures not bound to the land. Salmon migrate by combining celestial navigation with the use of olfactory nerves. Once I watched a determined salmon trying to make it up a clear, cold stream. The stream was so swift, I had trouble keeping my balance in it. The fish darted from an eddy behind a rock time and again, finally succeeding in advancing two feet. After ten more minutes, he had propelled himself another three feet. No doubt he battled on, foot by foot, inch by inch. He had come a hundred miles from the sea and had farther yet to go. All this effort was being expended so that the salmon could spawn in the stream of his birth. A fish cultivator with the Fisheries Rehabilitation and Enhancement Division put it this way: "Salmon figure, 'What's good enough for me is good enough for the kids.'" Billions of eggs and millions of fry are not successful in completing the full cycle of fresh water to salt water to fresh again. They run the gauntlet of predators: Dolly Varden trout, other fish, humans, birds, and marine life—all "lined up to chow down on them." Question marks remain about how to maintain the quality of sea and stream for these anadromous fish.

Many hardy seabirds thrive on other Pacific fish. The least auklet is a six-inch, black-and-white, stubby bird which nests on the cliffs of the Aleutian and Bering Sea islands. The islands of St. Lawrence and Little Diomede each have colonies numbering close to a million. The total auklet population is six million. And that is only *one* kind of bird.

All of Alaska's seacoasts and some of its inland waters host seabirds. While fishing commercially, Dale, a helper of ours, made the acquaintance of a lovely Arctic tern. This bird is a light gray-jacketed flier who not only dives swiftly for sticklebacks, but also can accurately dive-bomb an uncovered human head. Our cannery had anchored an old wooden barge offshore on which we deposited fish. The barge, painted many years before in timeless cannery yellow, a dark, golden-mud color, was so ancient it had grass growing in its cracks. Perhaps the terns viewed it as half-land, half-sea; whatever the reason, they nested there. Whenever we delivered fish, one of the terns would fly straight at Dale's bare head and strike a glancing blow hard enough to draw blood. Biologists who study birds have learned to wear a feather in their caps to ward off such nervous nesters.

To survive successfully in its habitat, each bird, like other animals, must possess its own niche. For example, puffins, auklets, and murrelets all dive easily, but they feed at different depths. They also have specialized nesting places: auklets nest in talus; horned puffins in burrows; and the marbled murrelet, it is thought, in trees. The common murre uses neither grass nor feathers, mud nor sticks. The bird simply lays an egg on bare rock. And an odd one it is, too; shaped a bit like a pear! It is this configuration that keeps many murre eggs from being destroyed when they are disturbed. The eggs whirl around, holding on to the ledge by their heavy end. When murre chicks are fledging, they flutter like leaves to the sea below. Virtually every time, they fall to the male parent who is somehow able to find them among hundreds of others.

There are more questions. How are the lives of sea birds affected by disease, storms, and the subsistence take of eggs? Disease becomes a suspect cause when one sees a bunch of healthy chicks one week and on return, finds them all dead. Scott Hatch, a specialist in sea birds, blames winter storms which can blow for weeks as a reason for large die-offs. The storms drive hundreds or thousands of sea birds from their usual feeding areas. When large groups of dead birds are found along a beach, one can look back in the meteorological records and often find weather as a cause.

The activities of fisheries can affect the lives of sea birds in two ways. First, the nine-mile-long gill nets of the Japanese high seas salmon fisheries unintentionally trap many marine mammals and birds, including the cormorant. Because this bird can dive more than one hundred feet for its prey, it frequently gets tangled deep in the nets. Then, indirect mortality of birds may occur in new, developing fisheries. Target species, such as squid, cod, and wall-eyed pollock, are the traditional staples of thick-billed murres and red-legged kittiwakes, birds that breed in the Aleutian, Pribilof, and Commander islands.

The fishery-bird conflict focuses on knowledge of what birds eat. To learn about the diet of the tufted puffin, Hatch and his associates placed a wire mesh barrier in front of the entrance to the puffin's burrow. The parent bird, unable to reach the chick, regurgitated its food, which was then collected and analyzed. The scientists found that, by weight, eighty to ninety percent of the food was made up of juvenile pollock. Since the Japanese fish for adult pollock, an easy solution to protecting the puffin would seem to be restricting the fishery. But this is not the entire picture. Adult pollock also eat their own juveniles. If the fishery restricted its take of adults, those remaining would prey more heavily on the juveniles, and *less* feed would be available to the puffins, rather than more. Nothing in biology is simple.

The watery world of the North Pacific is also a feeding ground for whales, seals, sea otters, and other marine mammals. Aside from the whale, the Pacific walrus is the largest marine mammal. Bulls can weigh thirty-five hundred pounds or more, making them as heavy as a pickup truck. Females are smaller. As adults, both sexes grow tusks, which are outsized canines of the upper jaw. As with land mammals, bulls of similar size engage in battles and sexual display. The walrus has a very light covering of hair on its body—unlike the furred or thick-haired seals—but is protected by thick blubber. When a walrus emerges from the cold water, he is often whitish or pinkish, an odd hue for such a large, tough-skinned fellow, who, out of water, is normally brown or brick red.

The walrus has a striking migration pattern. Breeding time is when the sea ice is at its southern extremity in the Bering Sea. After the female selects a displaying male, they copulate in the water. In the spring, as the ice begins to melt and retreat north toward the Chukchi Sea, the cows and their young follow it, accompanied by a few bulls. Birth takes place within this nursery herd on the ice. Newborn calves weigh a hefty 85 to 140 pounds. Many mature bulls move north into the Chukchi, too, but some—several thousand—often summer in the southeastern Bering Sea and along the northern Alaska Peninsula. Here they haul out on islands, gravel bars, and the coastal mainland. When cold weather returns and the ice pack reclaims the sea surface, the fall migration begins. Females and their young swim south before the advancing ice. Both sexes meet in their wintering grounds.

Walrus are primarily bottom feeders of clams, which they retrieve by suction. They "shell" the clam before eating it by sucking the clam's foot or siphon free of the shell.

The red squirrel, *Tamiasciurus hudsonicus*, often alerts other spruce forest animals to danger.

Like other breeding ungulates, bull moose "lip curl" in response to olfactory stimulation.

Since passage of the Marine Mammals Protection Act in 1972, only Alaska natives may harvest walrus in the United States. Formerly the big animals were hunted by sportsmen under state regulations. Commercial Soviet fleets also hunt the big pinniped. The walrus population of two hundred fifty to three hundred thousand is healthy, but some specialists believe walrus may be outstripping their supply of clams. Another concern about walrus has to do with their characteristic response to loud noise. While on haulouts, they make a rush for the water if disturbed. Many small walrus are trampled in the panic. For this reason, strict rules have been formulated for visiting and flying over walrus habitat.

Steller sea lions were named for the German who first identified them. They have no tusks and are less than half the size of a walrus. Their range is generally more southerly than that of the walrus, and they are more often found near the coast. The highest concentration of these sea lions is in the Gulf of Alaska, but some breed as far south as California. Sea lions do not show the walrus's marked drive to migrate, but they do disperse. Cows probably return to the rookery where they were born when they become pregnant.

In recent years, disturbing news has surfaced about the Steller sea lion. Their population in the eastern Aleutians is only about twenty-five percent of what it was seven years ago. This drop seems not to be due to an exodus of animals. A general decline has also been noted in other areas. Researchers who have been studying the mammals also find a large failure in the northern fur seal population. The fur seal was once the commercial mainstay of the Pribilof Islanders, but today it is no longer hunted except for subsistence. A drop in the harbor seal population around Kodiak from ten thousand to two thousand remains a mystery, too. Without further research, cautious biologists are reluctant to attribute the drop to any one cause. Some possible explanations include disease, a natural drop in the food supply, a reduction of pollock and cod by the commercial bottom fishery, entanglement in discarded fishing gear, and the ingestion of plastic waste material. The decline may also be the result of a combination of some of these factors.

Subsistence hunters in the far north prey on the adult bearded seal, or *oogruk*. This seal is generally gray or brownish, and lacks strong markings. Bearded seals and ringed seals are also the target of another hunter, the great white polar bear. This enormously strong carnivore will attack seals in a spring pupping den, patiently wait for them by a breathing hole, or hunt them at the ice's edge.

The polar bear lives in a world that expands in winter and diminishes under his feet in summer. Ice moves with the wind and current, riding the water uneasily. Much like the continents long ago, ice splits apart, but its rifts are called open leads and its mountain ranges, pressure ridges.

Ironically, most inhabitants of the forty-ninth state have seen their only polar bears in zoos. In Alaska, these bears roam the seas to the west and north. For centuries, Eskimos hunted polar bear; Alaskan Eskimos can still do so now without limit or seasonal constraint under subsistence regulations. This concerns some American and Canadian bear experts because of the animal's low reproductive potential. Some female polar bears may have only one or two litters in a lifetime.

Another issue of major concern is the expansion of industry and population to the Arctic. Polar bears find their primary prey in open leads. What will happen if a narrow sea lane in the ice is the site of a polluting spill?

Polar bears and brown/grizzly bears are of similar size, but its neck gives the white bear a stronger, thrusting appearance. Photographer Tom Walker, who has known a few bears pretty well, says, "As incredibly powerful as grizzlies can be, I think the polar bear must rank one notch above." He bases his opinion on observations of a drama acted out at a place most of us would consider the end of the world: the edge of a continent with only a frigid ocean lying beyond it.

In ending, I leave you with Tom's account of a polar bear and his remarkable photographs. Residents and former visitors alike will wonder, "How come that fellow Walker recalls my memories of Alaska so well?" Future visitors can take the pictures as assurance that someday they will round a bend in the trail and come upon similar sights. To the folks who will never make it physically to Alaska, count yourself in anyway. I can hear you singing, too.

Driven by a 40-mile-an-hour north wind, two miles of sea ice had been slammed to shore. Beyond it rolled a gray ice fog forming above open water. I took shelter and waited on a long graveled and rock-strewn spit thrust from the land by an Arctic river off to my left. On either side of the mouth, pressure ridges and a high ice wall stood sentry along the curving coast. Boulders there had repelled the attack of ocean breakers made sludgy with ice chunks half the size of a car. Cross-currents flowing from the river had opened large leads and patches of open water seething with spindrift. In them were thin river ice plates and more large blocks of frozen sea. I could hear grinding and crashing above the wind.

Then I saw the bear off to my right, making his way from land in a bid for the fog. Even the ice bear hesitates to venture head on into such a terrible wind. Surely he sought seals, hunger the one urge that couldn't be denied. In the fog he'd find his prey.

Soon his footing failed. He'd plunge in, pull himself out, jump from floe to floe, but oftentimes slid through openings in them and had to haul out to the larger ones.

The bear altered course and turned toward me, aiming for the spit and the river beyond. It was not a steady course change. He veered west, then tried north, then was forced south. Always he tested the ice to the north.

As he came closer, I'd see him for a while, then lose him behind a rolling wall of undulating ice. The pack was becoming more broken, and often the bear fought its way on, half swimming, half crawling. Several times he climbed out on huge frozen blocks and stood, staring north and west. I could see him rising and falling with the sea. When the bear met the battleground of ocean and river waters sluicing around the end of the point, he fell in among the masses of battering, churning floes; how could he keep from being crushed to death?

Just as I thought he must have perished, his head appeared at the top of one of the waves. He surfed toward shore and was flung against the white-encrusted boulders of the point, fighting to gain hold. In an instant, he washed back on an outflow of wave. Gone. Then he gained the ice wall, dug in with all four feet. Once ashore, he crossed in front of me and plunged into the river, swimming off to sea again by way of the fastest river current. He disappeared into the swirling ice fog, still heading north by northwest.

MARITIME

■ *Above*: *Enhydra lutris*, the sea otter, dives for food; upon surfac-
ing, it floats on its back while feeding. A tanner crab is smaller than
the more famous king crab. ■ *Right*: A marine member of the
weasel family, the sea otter has no thick blubber for insulation like a
seal. During the 1800s, the sea otter was overexploited for its thick fur.

■ *Left*: The world's largest breeding population of horned puffins—
between one and two million—is in Alaska. ■ *Above*: Puffin eggs
have been used as food by humans for centuries. In order to fly, the
bird must dive from cliffs, or when on water, "run" to become air-
borne. ■ *Overleaf*: When disturbed, walrus may erupt from a haul-
out area in a panicked dash for the sea, causing many calves to die.

■ *Above*: Walrus sleep in closely packed congregations. The genus name, *Odobenus*, means "tooth-walker," but although walrus can climb with the help of their tusks, they move by hoisting themselves along with hind limbs and front flippers. ■ *Right*: Haulouts are usually near supplies of bivalve molluscs, of which an adult walrus eats about one hundred thirty pounds daily.

■ *Left*: The extremely rare Aleutian Canada goose, *Branta canadensis leucopareia*, is identifiable by its white neck band. The fox is a major predator. ■ *Above*: *Ursus maritimus*, the polar bear, is a powerful hunter of seals. Study of the bears is made difficult by their seasonal movements and by changes in the distribution of the Arctic ice.

■ *Above*: Male polar bears are up to ten feet long. Females are smaller. In a radio-tracking experiment, they were usually found to den on the ice pack. ■ *Right*: Black-legged kittiwakes, here mixed in with gulls, recently suffered widespread reproductive failures in the Gulf of Alaska. Gull populations are healthy. ■ *Following page*: Sandpipers and plovers mix during spring migration.

■ *Left*: Arriving in the Pribilof Islands in May from their winter range in the Bering Sea, male northern fur seals, *Callorhinus ursinus*, will be joined later by females, some of whom have come from thousands of miles to the south. ■ *Above*: Birds breathe not only with lungs but with several membranous pockets in their wing bones which enable them to use extra oxygen on exhalation.

■ *Above*: Dark finned killer whales, *Orcinus orca*, are carnivorous mammals who may live to age forty. They can swim at twenty-five miles per hour. ■ *Right*: The long, rough bill of the red-faced cormorant, *Phalacrocorax urile*, clamps on a fish during a rapid dive to a depth of one hundred feet or more. But the bird is an awkward flier. The male cormorant's throat becomes blue during breeding.

■ *Left*: Blue phase pups exhibit a recessive gene of the Arctic fox, *Alopex lagopus*. ■ *Above*: Some red foxes, *Vulpes vulpes*, are bright orange-red, some are darker, a few are silver-tipped gray. Small mew gulls are prey for the fox. ■ *Overleaf*: The ten-ounce parakeet auklet, *Cyclorrhynchus psittacula*, nests deep in rock crevices.

■ *Above*: The common murre, *Uria aalge*, nests by the millions in colonies on steep cliffs in the Aleutians and along the Bering Sea coasts, where severe storms endanger the young in exposed nests.
■ *Right*: Northerly habitat is favored by the thick-billed murre, *Uria lomvia*. The nest site is bare rock, like that of the common murre, and both have high egg losses when disturbed.

■ *Left*: Steller sea lion females, *Eumetopias jubatus*, are bred ten days after giving birth to a single pup. Most sea lions in the Gulf of Alaska are born at only ten rookeries. Males reach their full weight, about twelve hundred fifty pounds, by age eleven. Females, mature at age eight, are half that size. ■ *Above*: Most feeding is done at night by *Rissa brevirostris*, the red-legged kittiwake.

■ *Above*: A glaucous-winged gull chick activates a regurgitation mechanism by touching the red spot on its parent's bill. During mating, females elicit the same response from males. ■ *Right*: Springtime flights by the crested auklet are seen in Kodiak and along the Bering Sea coasts. ■ *Following page*: Fierce competition prevents sea lion males from breeding before age eight.

■ *Left*: Preyed on by killer whales and polar bears, walrus are also hunted by Alaska Natives and Soviets, who prize both the meat and the ivory. ■ *Above*: In their search for molluscs, walrus root up the floor of the ocean with their whiskers.

FORESTS

■ *Above*: The female spruce grouse, *Canachites canadensis*, lacks the showy red eye comb of the cock in the spring. In the autumn, grouse seek out grit to process their winter food of spruce needles.
■ *Right*: Brown/grizzly bears generally prefer meadows and alpine areas to deep woods. Advice from experts is: never run from a wild animal, as it might trigger a pursuit response.

■ *Left*: A strip of velvet often persists on bull moose antlers.
■ *Above*: *Ursus americanus*, the black bear, feeds on horsetails from May to July in the Interior. On the Kenai Peninsula, prime habitat supports one bear per one and one-half square miles.
■ *Overleaf*: The predatory cat, *Lynx canadensis*, has been tracked for hundreds of miles following a sudden decrease of hare numbers.

■ *Above*: Large feet help the lynx bound in snow. Reports say it will chase a hare for only two hundred yards. ■ *Right*: Owls must turn their entire heads because their eyes cannot pivot. The great horned owl, *Bubo virginianus*, lives in old-growth forest, preying on rodents and other small mammals. Owls hoot and scream, but fly silently.

■ *Left*: American bison, *Bison bison*, is a species that has been transplanted to Alaska. Existing herds are not expected to increase much because the state has no areas of extensive grasslands.
■ *Above*: The few dark spots and the dark eyes indicate that the white moose is not an albino, yet an incidence of only two or three at any one time in the entire population shows its scarcity.

■ *Above*: The wing feathers of the black-billed magpie, *Pica pica*, are highly irridescent. Along with its cousin, the Canada jay, it is a frequent visitor to carrion sites. ■ *Right*: The short-tailed weasel, or ermine, *Mustela erminea*, is preyed on by raptors, coyotes, foxes, and lynx. ■ *Following page*: Silvery-green willow may find its way to the feed pile in the mouth of a beaver, *Castor canadensis*.

■ *Left*: Sharp hooves and great strength aid the cow moose in repelling wolf and black bear attacks. Usually, moose retreat from brown/grizzly bears. ■ *Above*: Fearless ravens, *Corvus corax*, attack a bald eagle, *Haliaeetus leucocephalus*. Such behavior, called "ganging," or "mobbing," is also practiced on other large, predatory birds.

■ *Above*: Fawns of the Sitka black-tailed deer, *Odocoileus hemionus sitkensis*, generally mature in the river drainages of their birth. Harsh winters regulate their numbers in dramatic fluctuation.
■ *Right*: The first fur to change to a mostly white winter coat on the snowshoe hare is on the top of its outsized hind feet.

■ *Left*: In the fall, female moose which are ready for breeding vocalize with a high descending moan. Bulls answer with a grunt.
■ *Above*: Slap of a beaver's tail sometimes signals danger. Beaver alter their habitat by turning streams into ponds, which eventually become meadows. ■ *Overleaf*: Bull moose, in their prime at age six to twelve years, may weigh twelve hundred pounds or more.

■ *Left*: A tranquil moose could change rapidly and charge; its head would lower, the hairs on its neck raise, and its ears lay flat.
■ *Above*: Antler growth in moose may be due in part to visitation in the spring at a mineral lick, where the principle element is sodium, although age and genetic factors may be the greatest influences.

■ *Above*: Hanging from behind the moose's chin is a dewlap, or "bell." This sack of hair-covered hide is common to both sexes. Hollow moose hair is a good insulator against cold, rain, frost, and snow. ■ *Right*: Young porcupine, *Erethizon dorsatum*, nurse at the soft, sparsely-haired underbelly of the mother. Only the most experienced predators try to attack the "porky." Most leave it alone.

■ *Left*: Beaver carefully monitor dams to provide the correct water level inside their lakeside lodges, because the beaver's home has dry benches along the inside walls. In the spring, the kits can be heard "mewing." ■ *Above*: Sound medical advice is to boil backcountry water to avoid the debilitating *giardiasis*, or "beaver fever," an intestinal complaint caused by a waterborne parasite.

MOUNTAINS

■ *Above*: On the Kenai Peninsula, mountain goats, *Oreamnos americanus*, do not visit mineral licks, but in the fall, they have been observed eating the roots of the false hellebore, a plant usually poisonous to sheep and definitely to man. ■ *Right*: Dall sheep in Alaska are estimated at seventy thousand. Bands of adult rams live apart from the ewes until the mating season in November and December.

■ *Left*: Bears verify visual information with their acute sense of smell. ■ *Above*: A bear's power is awesome, but it can be surprisingly gentle, especially in a female's play with her cubs. A bear's weight can vary by as much as a third from spring to autumn. "Hibernation" is any degree of dormancy, from a bear's lighter sleep state to the full hibernation of marmots and ground squirrels.

■ *Above*: Attention posture in a wild sheep is a stiff-legged, head-up stare, punctuated by wary glances to all sides. An alarmed sheep will bolt for the protection of nearby cliffs and peaks. ■ *Right*: Lambs are born singly in May or June in solitary mountain retreats. In the summer, while ewes travel downhill to feed, lambs gather in playful nursery groups which are often supervised by a single ewe.

■ *Left*: The dark slit below a dominant ram's eye marks a gland which is "horned," or rubbed, by young rams as part of a recognition process. ■ *Above*: In the Alaska range, whistles of the hoary marmot, *Marmota caligata*, warn Dall sheep of interlopers. ■ *Overleaf*: The posture of a dominant ram passing another of less prominence is one of many social interactions between wild sheep.

■ *Above*: The winter range of sheep is critical to their survival. Available on hills with a light covering of snow and on windswept ridges, dry grass and sedge are necessities—as are moss and lichen in some areas. ■ *Right*: Rock slopes are home to the collared pika, *Ochotona collaris*, tiny mammals of four to six inches. Members of the hare family, they usually live only three years.

■ *Left*: Ranging widely to find forage, caribou depend on climax vegetation of many years' growth. Groups sometimes join other herds, making enumeration difficult. ■ *Above*: Antler projection down over the caribou's nose is known as a "shovel"; some bulls have two. White necks and tails are highly visible on breeding animals.

TUNDRA

■ *Above*: Much of the Porcupine River herd of over one hundred fifty thousand caribou winters in Canada and calves in Alaska's Arctic National Wildlife Range. ■ *Right*: Swans of reproductive age will take a new mate if one dies. Tundra swans, *Olor columbianus*, favor the western tundra habitat for nesting. ■ *Following page*: The red fox possesses sharp senses of smell, hearing, and sight.

■ *Left*: Summer plumage of the willow ptarmigan is speckled. The eggs are a spotted, rich red, and males help with chick rearing. In the winter, the ptarmigan dives into the snow at night for warmth.
■ *Above*: In a rain storm, a drenched red fox hunts rodents, probably a vole; when sated, the fox will store food for future meals.

■ *Above*: The biggest asset of *Canis lupus*, the wolf, is the social structure of the pack, whose members cooperate in hunting ventures. Wolves eat four to seven pounds of meat daily. A lone wolf may be a non-breeding male, a young wolf in search of new territory, or a pack member that is hunting alone. ■ *Right*: A caribou in its prime can outrun both bears and wolves.

■ *Left*: In the winter, the line from eye to beak is characteristic of the male rock ptarmigan, *Lagopus mutus*, which eats willow and dwarf birch. ■ *Above*: The neck and head feathers of the oldsquaw drake change to black in the fall. ■ *Overleaf*: The muskox, *Ovibos moschatus*, a species reintroduced in the 1930s to Alaska, meets predators in a defensive line or circle.

■ *Above*: The cow caribou is the only female deer to grow antlers, but pregnant cows drop them in early spring. Calves weigh about thirteen pounds at birth, and can stand up in a few minutes.
■ *Right*: Among the red leaves of autumn dwarf birch, blueberries, and alpine bearberries are lichens and sedges, the caribou's primary cold-weather food.

■ *Left*: On the tundra, remains of animals are food for many creatures. Horns, antlers, and bones are chewed by shrews, porcupines, foxes, and others. Without the three-inch bone beneath their horns, muskoxen would injure their brains during breeding clashes.
■ *Above*: The velvet on antlers, actually a skin containing blood vessels which nourish the young antlers, is rubbed off before breeding.

■ *Above*: A hunter and smallest of the jaegers, the long-tailed jaeger, *Stercorarius longicaudus*, will attack intruders after a noisy warning and spread-wing display. ■ *Right*: Caribou are circumpolar animals which are descended from herds of the Pleistocene. ■ *Following page:* Antlers of older caribou are more irregular than are those of a bull in its prime. Female antlers are small.

■ *Left*: In its dry hilltop terrain, *Spermophilus parryii*, the Arctic ground squirrel, hibernates in the winter; in summer, it eats a variety of plants, as well as eggs, insects, and carrion. ■ *Above*: Joined by flocks from Siberia, the autumn migration of gray Sandhill cranes, *Grus canadensis*, signals that winter is close.

WATERS

■ *Above*: The incidence of three cubs is not unusual. Rough-and-tumble young brown/grizzly bears stay with the female until her next estrus cycle or leave in their third or fourth spring. In contrast, black bear families split up in the second year. ■ *Right*: Spring and early summer use of lowland ponds and muskegs by moose give way in August to browsing at higher elevations.

■ *Left*: Red salmon, or "sockeyes," leap the falls in an unrelenting return to their spawning grounds. ■ *Above*: Ripe female chum salmon eggs are tossed into the air as the fish and internal roe sac are shaken. ■ *Overleaf*: Fishing styles vary among bears, but most trap fish with their feet, then grab them with their mouths. Chum salmon, *Onchorhynchus keta*, are noted for their deeply V-ed tails.

■ *Above*: No longer considered rare in Alaska, trumpeter swans, *Olor buccinator*, usually migrate in families. They are best known for their call which resembles the sound of a hunting horn. ■ *Right*: In the Interior, mountain lakes near timberline are rimmed with small spruces and shrub willow. Stream banks at higher levels and in Arctic regions are also hosts to willow, which is eaten by moose.

■ *Left*: The national symbol of the United States, the mature bald eagle sports a clearly defined white head and tail. ■ *Above*: Birds of prey, eagles grasp food in their talons while feeding or in flight. Pesticides have shown up in some Alaskan bald eagles.

■ *Above*: As male brown bears grow older and larger, they tend to darken, probably from the hormone, testosterone. Because such bears sometimes kill and eat young bears, their dark color may be a visual symbol of danger. ■ *Right*: Three to four weeks of molt during early summer leave *Branta canadensis parvipes*, the lesser Canada goose, and other waterfowl flightless and open to attack.

■ *Left*: More adaptable than Dall sheep and caribou, moose can do well in a variety of habitats, especially on land recovering from fire.
■ *Above*: The white patch of the forewing barely shows on a drifting American widgeon, *Anas americana*. It is noticeable on individual ducks in flocks as they turn and twist in flight. Some widgeons summer in Anchorage on the world's largest float plane base.

■ *Above*: By agitating the rock and water with their tails, red salmon—named for their bright flesh—prepare a "redd," or nest, in the streambed. Earlier in the season, the fish are silvery. ■ *Right*: Biologists figure bears' ages by examination of the cementum layers on their teeth. Some bears live into their twenties. Taxidermists report that often age and injury have deformed bear skulls.

■ *Left*: Yawning is often a sign of low level stress in bears, brought on by close proximity to other bears or humans. In viewing areas, efforts are made to minimize stress. ■ *Above*: After earnest rearing by parent birds, bald eaglets leave the nest in late summer. Their immature plumage lasts for three or four years. Old growth trees, which may be two hundred years old, are critical habitat for them.

■ *Above*: The population of bald eagles in Alaska is strong, although the bird is considered endangered in states to the south. In the treeless Aleutians, the bald eagle must nest on cliffs or on the ground. ■ *Right*: Adult bears, like cubs, sometimes play-fight. Most encounters are settled by open-mouth displays, elaborate body language, or outright flight. Females defend their cubs fiercely.

■ *Left*: One of six subspecies of Canada geese in the state, the lesser Canada goose is of medium size. In the air, geese can be distinguished from ducks by their deeper, slower wing beats. ■ *Above*: Spring nesting lesser Canada geese choose pond marshes in various parts of Alaska. They may be viewed easily at Potter Marsh in Anchorage along Alaska's major Highway 1.

■ *Above*: The population of brown/grizzly bears is high in Alaska, but estimates are unreliable. Disturbance of their habitat is the major threat to these generally reclusive and solitary animals of the wild forests, mountains, and tundra. ■ *Right*: Gulls are opportunistic feeders and follow predatory animals to share in their kills, sometimes even perching on the backs of bears.

■ *Left*: In the spring, horsetails and pondweeds comprise some of the thirty to fifty pounds of daily vegetation needed by a moose.
■ *Above*: The alarm call of three or four cries—repeated quickly and for as long as intruders are visible—is a sign of the greater yellowlegs, also known for swinging their bills in the water.

■ *Above*: *Anas acuta*, or northern pintail, is the most abundant of the twelve million ducks which nest in Alaska. The color of the hens is more subdued than is that of the drakes. Pintails are slim, dabbling ducks which consume plant seeds and greens, as well as pond invertebrates. ■ *Right*: Trails of the hardy moose lead like spokes to the hubs of Alaska's many ponds. Moose are powerful swimmers.

■ *Left*: Interior Alaska has a large concentration of trumpeter swans. Their bodies measure five feet in length; their eggs, five inches.
■ *Above*: A green head identifies the mallard drake, *Anas platyrhynchos*. Less conspicuous, except in flight, is the blue speculum, a patch of color found on the wings of both sexes. The hen emits a loud quack as compared to the drake's quieter call.

■ *Above*: Even while at rest, the raven's high metabolic rate enables it to withstand Alaska's cold winter temperatures. ■ *Right*: Through the centuries, bears have weathered many natural phenomena like the 1986 Mt. Augustine eruption. Although Alaska's bears are potentially dangerous to man, human intolerance of bears, says a biologist studying them, is much more common than the other way around.

AUTHOR'S ACKNOWLEDGEMENTS

The author gratefully acknowledges the assistance of the following people in the completion of this project:

Steve Amstrup, Larry Aumiller, Ted Bailey, Eric Beeman, Red Beeman, Eric Braendel, Dr. Bryant, Bruce Campbell, David Cline, Don Caulkins, Jim Davis, Barrie Gilbert, Dave Harkness, Scott Hatch, Wayne Heimer, Pauline Hessing, Ben Hilliker, Dave Holderman, Dan Holleman, Ed Holstein, Jim Kaplan, Ray Kramer, Sterling Miller, Dennis Money, Lyman Nichols, Leonard Oakley, Ken Pitcher, Keith Pratt, Nancy Tankersley, Thede Tobish, Lance Trasky.